Published by HarperCollins*Entertainment* 2000
An Imprint of HarperCollins*Publishers* Ltd
77-85 Fulham Palace Road, London W6 8JB
First published in the USA by
Random House Inc, New York, USA 2000

ISBN 0 00 710340 9
1 3 5 7 9 8 6 4 2
Printed and bound in Belgium by Proost

www.universalstudios.com
The HarperCollins website address is:
www.**fire**and**water**.com

Dr. Seuss' How the Grinch Stole Christmas!

Grinch & Bear It!

Life According to the Supreme Green Meanie!

Based on the
motion picture screenplay by
Jeffrey Price & Peter S. Seaman

Based on the book by Dr. Seuss

HarperCollins*Entertainment*
An imprint of HarperCollins*Publishers*

"The term *Grinchy* will apply
when Christmas spirit is in short supply."
—*The Book of Who*

Sometime in the years after the publication of Dr. Seuss' classic *How the Grinch Stole Christmas!*, the word *grinch* entered our language as a term meaning "a person or thing that spoils or dampens the pleasure of others." (It's in Webster's—you can look it up!) In other words, it describes someone who indulges in stingy, "bah, humbug type" behavior, just as the Grinch did when he stole Christmas from the citizens of Whoville.

When Theodor Geisel—better known as Dr. Seuss—wrote his best-selling book in 1957, he meant it as a cautionary message to all of us. He was saying that we were losing sight of the true meaning of

Christmas. The holiday, which had begun as a joyous religious celebration, was becoming hopelessly buried under an onslaught of crass commercialization. The joyous themes of Christmas past had become—as personified by the Whos' pre-holiday frenzy—buy, buy, buy and spend, spend, spend.

How the Grinch Stole Christmas! shows us, through Cindy Lou Who's innocent faith and the Grinch's transformation, that we mustn't forget the true meaning and spirit of Christmas as a time for giving—of ourselves and our love—to others.

Dr. Seuss' *How the Grinch Stole Christmas!* is a magical story that has been transformed into a brilliant comic movie with heart and with a universal message about goodness and generosity at a time when such a message is needed more sorely than ever.

Here's to the true spirit of Christmas!

—*The Editors*

ON BEING A WHO

No matter how different
a Who may appear,
he'll always be welcomed
with Holiday Cheer.

—*The Book of Who*

Every size of Who
we can measure
knows that Whobilation
is a time we must treasure.

—*The Book of Who*

The Cheermeister is one who deserves
a cheer, a backslap, or a toast!
It goes to the soul at Christmas
who needs it most.

—*The Book of Who*

Since Christmas cards are sent by mail
the Postal Service must never fail.

—*The Book of Who*

ON THE WHO-LETIDE

We've got to keep shop-shop-shopping!

—*Lou Lou Who*

That's what it's always been about,
isn't it? Gifts! Gifts! Gifts! Well, let me
tell you what happens to your gifts:
They all end up coming to me...
in your garbage...at the dump!

—*The Grinch to the assembled Whos*

This is my favorite day of the year:
three days before Christmas!...
Then, of course, there's two days
before Christmas—and Christmas Eve...
Then again, there's Christmas itself...
Then again, there's the day *after* Christmas!
You know what? They're all great!

—Lou Lou Who

Now let's just concentrate on having the best
Christmas ever!

—Mayor May Who

ON THE WHOBILATION

I tell you people *one* thing:
Invite the Grinch, destroy Christmas.
But did anyone listen?

—Mayor May Who

I just wanted everyone to be together for Christmas.

—Cindy Lou Who

Who knows? This Whobilation could change my entire outlook on life.

—The Grinch

Well…if you Lou Whos have finished desecrating the most important day of the year, maybe now we can all get back to Christmas the way it should be—Grinchless.

—Mayor May Who

They'll bang on ting-tinglers
and blow their floo-flounders;
they'll bash their jing-jinglers
and bounce on boing-bounders.

—The Grinch

Nutcracker! It's their Whobilation! I can't watch another minute of this.

—The Grinch

TO HIS FAITHFUL DOG, MAX

Fleas before beauty.

—*The Grinch*

Hello, Max. Are you having a holly jolly Christmas?

—*The Grinch*

All right! You're a reindeer. Here's your motivation: You're Rudolph, you're different, you can't play any reindeer games. Then Santa picks you and you save Christmas—wait, no you don't, forget that part. We'll improvise. You *hate* Christmas; you're going to steal it. Saving Christmas was a lousy ending, totally unrealistic. And…Action!

—*The Grinch*

I don't know why you're laughing, Rudolph...

—*The Grinch*

Work it, Max. Feel the burn. All you!

—*The Grinch*

ON HEARTS

Look, it's the size of a baby pea!

—The Grinch on the state of his heart

O bleeding hearts of the world unite!

—The Grinch

Oh, no, Max,
help me!
I'm...
FEELING!

—The Grinch

What's happened to me? I'm all toasty inside. Oh, Max…I love you.

—*The Grinch*

ON THE MAKING OF A GRINCH

We knew
right away
he was…special.
—*Clarinella*

He was a
wonderful little…
whatever-he-was…
—*Clarinella*

My, haven't
you turned
out to be
a handsome,
odd-looking
whatever-
you-are!
—*Clarinella*

{The Grinch} is a what who just doesn't like Christmas.

—*Lou Lou Who*

Santa?
Don't forget
the Grinch.
I know he's
mean and hairy
and smelly.
His hands
may be cold
and clammy.
But I think
he's actually
kinda…sweet.

—*Cindy Lou*

ON BEING A GRINCH

I've got to do something.
Those Whos have to pay.

—*The Grinch*

How dare you enter the Grinch's lair?!? You little micro-menace! The impudence! The audacity! The unmitigated gall! You will rue the day you came here! You called down the thunder; now get ready for the Boom. Gaze into the face of fear!!!!!

—*The Grinch to Cindy Lou*

All right, Whoville, if you're hungry for humbug, I'm the special of the day!… and I deliver!

—*The Grinch*

ON BEING GRINCHY

Four Whos, one Grinch. I'll take those odds...

—*The Grinch*

Serves them right,
those yuletide-loving,
sickly sweet,
nog-sucking
cheermongers.
I mean, I really
don't like 'em.
Mm-mm, no,
I don't.

—*The Grinch*

Fat Boy should be finishing up any time now. Talk about a recluse. He only comes out once a year—you don't see him catching any flak...

—*The Grinch*

Ya got me, Officer. I did it. I am the Grinch who stole Christmas and I'm sorry. Don't you want to cuff me? Put me in a choke hold. How about pepper spray? I deserve it. I'm a loose cannon. I'm a live wire. I'm a threat to society!

—*The Grinch*

GRINCH-ISMS

Be it ever so heinous,
there's no place like home.
—*The Grinch*

Right...
See, the North Pole's
being renovated.
So I'm working out of
the South Pole this year.
Got a little time-share with
the Tooth Fairy and, you know,
Sasquatch. Good guy. I gotta go.
—*The Grinch*

And now for the final brushstroke
of my stinky rotten masterpiece
of...not-niceness!
Oh, the wailing
and the gnashing of teeth!
It'll be music to my ears!
—*The Grinch*

Nothing like a little snowball fight
to break the ice.

—*The Grinch*

You see, Max, one man's compost heap is
another man's potpourri.

—*The Grinch*

ON THE TRUE MEANING OF CHRISTMAS

Christmas is about being together with our families and loved ones. And that's all. Everything else is...superfluous. And that means *unnecessary*.

—*Lou Lou Who*

I don't need presents. What more could I want for Christmas than this?

—*Lou Lou Who*

Because that's not what Christmas is really all about, gifts and contests and fancy lights...

—*Lou Lou Who*

Merry Christmas, Cindy Lou!

—The Grinch

Welcome Christmas...Fa-Who-Ra-Mus!
Christmas Day is in our grasp...
As long as we have hands to clasp...

—*The Whos*

Merry Christmas, Betty Lou. I have absolutely nothing more to give you.

—*Lou Lou Who*

MERRY CHRISTMAS, MR. GRINCH!

I came to see you. No one should be alone on Christmas.

—*Cindy Lou Who to the Grinch*